Saint Clare of Assisi

Saint Clare of Assisi
A Light for the World

Written by Marianne Lorraine Trouvé, FSP
Illustrated by Mary Joseph Peterson, FSP

Pauline
BOOKS & MEDIA
Boston

Library of Congress Cataloging-in-Publication Data

Trouvé, Marianne Lorraine.
  Saint Clare of Assisi : a light for the world / written by Marianne Lorraine Trouvé ; illustrated by Mary Joseph Peterson.
     p. cm. — (Encounter the saints series ; 26)
  ISBN 0-8198-7122-2 (pbk.)
1. Clare, of Assisi, Saint, 1194-1253—Juvenile literature. 2. Christian saints—Italy—Assisi—Biography—Juvenile literature. 3. Assisi (Italy)—Biography—Juvenile literature. I. Peterson, Mary Joseph. II. Title.
  BX4700.C6T76 2009
  271'.97302—dc22
  [B]
                              2009008646

"P" and PAULINE are registered trademarks of the Daughters of St. Paul.

Published by Pauline Books & Media, 50 Saint Pauls Avenue, Boston, MA 02130-3491

Printed in the U.S.A.

www.pauline.org

SCOA VSAUSAPEOILL7-25J13-06796 7122-2

Pauline Books & Media is the publishing house of the Daughters of St. Paul, an international congregation of women religious serving the Church with the communications media.

2 3 4 5 6 7 8 9   17 16 15 14 13

Encounter the Saints Series

Blesseds Jacinta and Francisco Marto
Shepherds of Fatima

Blessed John Paul II
The People's Pope

Blessed Pier Giorgio Frassati
Journey to the Summit

Blessed Teresa of Calcutta
Missionary of Charity

Journeys with Mary
Apparitions of Our Lady

Saint Anthony of Padua
Fire and Light

Saint Bakhita of Sudan
Forever Free

Saint Bernadette Soubirous
And Our Lady of Lourdes

Saint Catherine Labouré
And Our Lady of the Miraculous Medal

Saint Clare of Assisi
A Light for the World

Saint Damien of Molokai
Hero of Hawaii

Saint Edith Stein
Blessed by the Cross

Saint Elizabeth Ann Seton
Daughter of America

Saint Faustina Kowalska
Messenger of Mercy

Saint Frances Xavier Cabrini
Cecchina's Dream

CONTENTS

A LIGHT FOR THE WORLD

Lady Ortolana Offreduccio stopped in the middle of the hot, dusty road. Breathing hard, she bent over slightly, pushing aside the wisps of hair clinging to her damp face.

Her two ladies-in-waiting, distant relatives of the noblewoman, sprang to her side.

"My lady, let me help you," said one.

"Thank you, Pacifica," murmured Lady Ortolana. "Normally I don't mind the heat. But now, with the baby due so soon, I need to rest a bit."

The three women were walking to the nearby Cathedral of San Rufino in Assisi, Italy. Ortolana wanted to pray that she would give birth to a healthy baby.

"Don't worry, my lady," said Bona, the other lady-in-waiting. "We will be at the church soon. God will hear your prayers for a safe delivery."

Ortolana smiled. Her husband, Lord Favarone, had beamed with joy when she told him she was expecting their first baby. Since then she had prayed often for their child.

Soon the women entered the cathedral.

"I want to pray in front of the crucifix," Ortolana whispered. Her long gown rustled as she knelt down, her eyes fixed on Jesus on the cross. *Lord, watch over and protect this child of mine. Give me a safe delivery. May the child be healthy and come to know and love you.*

Ortolana was filled with the love of Jesus. A great sense of peace came over her. Then, in her heart, she suddenly heard the words, "You will bear a child who shall be a light for all the world."

Startled, she looked up at the cross. *Lord, was that you?*

Ortolana pondered the words, repeating them over and over in her mind. *You will bear a child who shall be a light for all the world.*

What could it mean?

A few weeks later, in the summer of 1194, Lady Ortolana gave birth. The cries of a newborn baby girl filled the room. Tears rolled down Ortolana's face as she cradled her daughter to her heart and showed the child to Favarone.

"What shall we call her?" he asked.

"Clare. It means light—brilliant light."

Ortolana again thought of the words she had heard in the church: "You will bear a child who shall be a light for all the world." As she looked at the tiny baby, now quietly sleeping, she wondered again what it all meant.

Word about the new baby's name quickly spread. "What a beautiful name!" Pacifica and Bona told each other as they bustled around the house. "A beautiful name for a beautiful baby!"

They loved helping Lady Ortolana care for the little girl. By the time Clare was three-and-a-half years old, another baby, Catherine, was born. Two years later, a third daughter, Beatrice, made her appearance. Lady Ortolana's joy was complete!

The three girls grew up in a happy household. In the large Offreduccio villa in the hill town of Assisi, the family lived a life of luxury. The children were very happy as they played. But outside the villa, serious problems were brewing.

A civil war had broken out in Assisi. Many of the poorer people were angry at the wealthier, noble families. There was fighting in the streets. Villas and castles were attacked. Clare's parents talked about what they should do.

"Ortolana," said Favarone. "It's too dangerous to stay here. The mobs may attack our house—burn it—and even kill us!"

"What shall we do?" cried Ortolana, with tears in her eyes.

"We must flee to Perugia. It's not too far away, but we'll be safe there."

"Oh, Favarone," said Ortolana, "I hate to leave our lovely home in Assisi!"

"Don't worry, Ortolana," he replied. "As soon as peace comes again, we'll return."

So the family fled to Perugia, fifteen miles away, for safety. The older girls cried as they left, sad to leave their friends and their home. Their house in Assisi was indeed damaged in the riots, but fortunately it wasn't burned. After several years in Perugia, the Offreduccios were able to return. Finally, they were home again!

2

THE MARKET OF ASSISI

Twelve-year-old Clare skipped down the cobbled street, followed by Catherine. They loved visiting the markets and shops of Assisi with their mother. Colorful mounds of fruits and vegetables glowed against the pale stone walls. The streets were alive with busy shoppers, shouting vendors, donkeys, horses, and the occasional stray dog. The Offreduccio girls enjoyed it all!

"Mama, look!" Clare cried. "There, across the street, is the beggar I told you about. I want to help him. May I give him some food?"

A frail, elderly man sat by the street, covered with a tattered cloak. As people walked by, he looked up to plead with them. "Can you spare some food for me, for the love of our Lord, Jesus Christ?"

Clare tugged at her mother's silk dress. "Please, Mama, can I give him something?"

Her mother replied, "Yes, Clare, take some of this bread I just bought and give it to him. God has given us many blessings, so we ought to share with the poor."

"Thank you, Mama," Clare shouted as she took the loaf and ran across the street.

She approached the beggar and offered him the loaf of bread. "Please take it for the love of Jesus Christ," she told him.

The beggar looked up at the little girl with the golden hair. He reached out his hand and took the loaf. "Thank you, my little one" he told her. "May God reward you!" The bread was hardly in his hand before he began to devour chunks of it.

"Stay with me, girls," said Ortolana. "I need to visit this shop to price some silk for a new dress. I won't be buying anything today, though, so it shouldn't take long."

They entered a shop where they saw a young man measuring bolts of cloth. When Ortolana and her daughters entered, he approached them with a bow. "Can I interest you lovely ladies in some of the finest cloth in all of Assisi?" he asked with a smile.

Ortolana looked at the brightly colored cloth and thought of new curtains ... new bed hangings ... and ...

"Francis Bernardone, I must admit it's tempting!" she exclaimed. "I hadn't intended to buy anything, but ..."

"Lady Offreduccio, surely a lovely lady like you will want some lovely cloth for your home."

Ortolana shook her head, laughing. "It's hard to say no to you, Francis!" she replied. She chose her cloth and paid the young man. Clare was watching him intently.

Francis caught her eye. "I'm a lucky man! It is not every day that such a beautiful princess comes to our shop! What's your name?" he asked.

Clare smiled shyly. "I'm not a princess! My name is Clare!"

"You certainly look like a princess to me!" Francis replied. "Let's play a game. See this coin in my hand?" He held out his hand. A large coin was in his palm. "Watch it disappear!" He closed his fingers over his palm, then opened them up again. The coin was gone!

"How did you do that?" Clare cried.

"A magician never tells the secret!" Francis laughed.

"All right, Clare," Mama said. "Enough magic tricks for today! It's time to go home."

"How did you do that?"

One night several years later, Clare and her family were eating dinner.

"Did you hear what happened today?" her father asked.

Everyone looked at him. "No, Father, what is it?" Clare asked.

"It's the talk of the town!" Favarone said. "That young Francis Bernardone has made a total fool of himself!"

"Why?" Ortolana asked. "Whatever did he do?"

"His father dragged him before the bishop and accused Francis of stealing from him. Francis admitted it was true. He took some cloth from his father's shop and sold it. He wanted to give the money to the poor. But the bishop told him it wasn't right to steal. He said that Francis should give back the money."

"So did he do that?" Catherine asked.

"Yes, but not only that!" Favarone said. "Francis not only gave the money back, he also took off his clothes—since his father had paid for them—and gave those back, too! The bishop had to wrap Francis in a cloak!"

Clare's eyes grew big. "So Francis has nothing at all?" she asked.

"He wants nothing at all!" her father said. "Now he's going around Assisi preaching to people. Francis keeps talking about something crazy—being Christ's knight—and serving Lady Poverty."

"I wonder what he means by that," Clare said. "Lady Poverty ..." She grew thoughtful and finished her dinner in silence.

3

A Marriage Proposal

At seventeen, Clare was becoming a lovely young woman. One Sunday, coming out of church after Mass, she passed two young men. "Look how beautiful she is!" one of them exclaimed. "Her golden hair, her exquisite face, her kind expression ... "

"I know what you mean," the other replied. "When she looks at me, I feel as though her eyes can see my very soul."

As Clare walked home with her family, her mother said, "Clare, it's time for you to start thinking about your future. Consider Lord Ranieri di Bernardo. He's a distant cousin and a fine young man, and he would make a good husband for you."

Clare's heart sank. "Mother," she said, "I've already told you—I'm not planning to get married. Jesus Christ, the Son of God, has already won my heart."

"That's ridiculous!" Ortolana sputtered. "You must marry into a good family, with plenty of money to support you. We want you to be comfortable. We certainly can't have you living in poverty!"

"Poverty," Clare whispered under her breath. She had heard someone else speak about poverty. But it was in a very different way. She reminded her mother, "Brother Francis Bernardone walks the streets of Assisi and talks about poverty. He says it's the best way to become close to God."

"Your mother and I don't want you listening to that crazy Francis anymore," her father cried. "What a disappointment he turned out to be! Everyone thought he would become a cloth merchant like his father. But then he got those ridiculous ideas in his head. Now other young men have joined him. They call themselves friars and they talk about poverty. Poverty! As if having nothing to eat and no place to stay are what God wants for us!"

"But Francis teaches about the ways of God, Father," Clare replied gently.

"Nonsense! He and his followers! Why, they're just as crazy as he is! They go around Assisi wearing old rags and begging for food. I don't want you to have anything to do with them. It's bad enough that your cousin Rufino joined Francis and his new religious order."

Clare kept silent. She knew it was useless to argue with her father, especially about this.

"Now, Clare," her mother continued, "listen to me. Lord Ranieri will be having supper with us tonight, and I want you to be polite to him."

"Yes, Mother, of course I will be polite."

That evening Clare heard a knock on the door. A maid answered it, and Ranieri stepped into the house. Immediately he spotted Clare and walked up to her, then bowed with a sweep of his hand.

"Lady Clare," he announced. "I am honored to be in your presence." He reached for her hand and kissed it.

"Welcome, Lord Ranieri," she responded. "The table is ready, and my parents are looking forward to seeing you."

After dinner Ranieri asked Clare, "May I walk with you outside in the gardens?"

"Yes, of course," she replied. They stepped outside into the warm night air. The stars were just starting to light up the sky. The flowers swayed in a gentle breeze, sending their delicate scent wafting over the orderly shrubs and bushes.

As they walked, Ranieri's heart began to beat faster. The right moment had arrived. He had to ask her now. "Let's sit on that bench," he suggested. His mouth felt dry as he searched for the right words.

"Lady Clare, you are the most beautiful woman in all of Assisi. For so long I've dreamed about what it would be like to be with you all the time."

A look of concern passed over Clare's face. She knew what was coming.

"Clare," he continued, "will you marry me?"

Clare took a deep breath. She thought about what to say. She didn't want to hurt him, but she had to be firm.

"Ranieri," she began, "I have long admired you, too. You are indeed a fine man and will make an excellent husband one day—for some lucky girl. But not for me. I've already pledged my heart to another."

His face fell. *Who could she mean?* he thought. *Who could she like better than me?* "Clare, I didn't know that you were already engaged to be married!" he cried.

"I am not engaged to be married."

Ranieri looked puzzled. "I don't understand," he said. "If you aren't engaged, why refuse me?"

"Ranieri, I've pledged my heart to Jesus Christ. He is my one true love and will be my heavenly spouse."

So that's it! She's going to enter a convent! he thought. He pleaded with her. "Clare, I'll love you forever! You can marry me and love God, too," he argued.

"Ranieri, it's true that marriage is a holy calling. But Jesus isn't calling me to marriage. He wants something different of me. He wants me to give my heart to him alone—in a special way. This is the path he wants me to travel with him. I've already told him yes, I will do that. So I cannot marry you. If you knew the God who loves us so much, you would want to give him your heart, too."

The determination in her gentle voice told Ranieri that it would be useless to talk about it anymore. With a heavy heart, he got up and left. As he rode away on his horse, Clare breathed a sigh of relief. But what would her parents say now?

4

TROUBLE AT HOME

"You told him no?" Lord Favarone shouted. "What's gotten into you, Clare? Ranieri is from a fine family! He'd make you a good husband. How could you say no?"

Clare's voice trembled, but she spoke clearly. "Father, I cannot marry him. My heart is pledged to another."

"Another? Who? What are you talking about?" he demanded.

Clare drew a deep breath. "I cannot marry any man on this earth, for my heart is pledged to Jesus Christ."

Favarone shook his head in disbelief. "This will pass, Clare. Right now your head is filled with strange ideas. But soon enough you'll forget about them. You will marry. If not Ranieri, then another young man from a good family."

Suddenly he pounded his fist on the table. "I'll never allow you to run off to a convent!" With that he got up and left.

Clare's face turned pink. She knew what God wanted her to do, and she was determined to do it. But she needed to clear her thoughts. She went to walk in the garden. What should she do next? Just then an idea popped into her head. *Francis!* she thought. *I should go and talk to Brother Francis! He'll show me what to do.*

The next day she had to go into Assisi to do some shopping for her mother. *When I get there I'll look for him and ask if I can speak to him,* she thought.

As she went into the town, she looked down each street. Francis and his brothers spent their days walking through Assisi, preaching and singing. Finally, Clare glimpsed Francis in his gray, patched robe.

"Brother Francis," she began, "I know you are a holy man of God. Can I please speak to you about something very important?"

"Certainly, Lady Clare," he replied. "Come into the church." Francis and another brother walked with Clare into the entryway of the church. She began to spill out her whole heart to them.

"I know that Jesus is calling me to follow him in a special way. But my parents want me to get married instead. Until now I've managed to say no to them. But they are losing patience. I'm afraid they will force me into a marriage I don't want."

Francis nodded his head. He stayed quiet for a moment. Then he said, "I can help you."

He stroked his beard. "Tell me exactly what it is you want," he asked.

"I want to follow Jesus Christ and give myself to him," Clare told him. "I want to live a poor, simple life. I don't want to have a big house, a lot of money, or servants. I want to live as you do."

Francis was overjoyed. "Clare," he began, "this is just what I was hoping for. I already have a place in mind where you can live. It's at the Church of San Damiano, just outside Assisi."

Clare's eyes lit up. She replied, "Francis, I heard about how you worked to repair that church. One day you told some friends of mine that a group of holy women would come to live there, right near the church."

Francis smiled. "Yes, it's true. But we must not rush into anything. I'd like to meet with you over some time. We can discuss this more, little by little, and in prayer see what the Lord is asking us to do."

Nodding her head in agreement, Clare got up. They decided on a time and a place to meet next. Excited yet anxious, Clare wondered, *What will this all lead to?*

5

A GRIEVING FAMILY

Lady Ortolana was crying. Her sobs echo-ed through the house. When Clare heard them, she rushed to be with her mother.

"Mother!" she cried. "What's wrong? Why are you crying?"

Blinking through her tears, Ortolana said, "Your father is dying! He suddenly collapsed after he had finished eating. The servants have carried him upstairs."

"Has someone sent for the priest?" Clare asked.

"Yes, one of the servants went. He should be here soon."

Clare rushed upstairs to her father's room. He was lying on the bed. His eyes were closed. He was breathing only with great effort.

She knelt down next to the bed and took his hand. "Father! Father!" she cried. "Please don't die! We don't want to lose you."

He struggled to open his eyes. When he saw Clare, he squeezed her hand.

"Chiarita," he said, using his affectionate name for her. "Chiarita ..." His voice faded.

Tears flowed down Clare's face. He was struggling again, trying to say something.

"Take care of your mother."

"Yes, Father, I will."

Just then the priest came in. He brought with him a small vessel that contained the Blessed Sacrament. The family withdrew while the priest heard Favarone's final confession. After the absolution, the priest gave Favarone his last Holy Communion. Then he told the family to come back inside.

Ortolana, Clare, Catherine, and Beatrice all gathered around Favarone's bedside. For the final time, his eyes closed. His breathing stopped. He was gone.

What would happen to them now? How would life go on?

6

CLARE'S PLAN OF ACTION

After her father's death, Clare grieved. *How brief life is!* she thought. *I'll live on earth a few years, and then I, too, will die and be with God.* Clare found herself thinking more and more about the purpose of life. During the next year, she met often with Francis. When he spoke to her about the love of Jesus Christ, Clare's heart burned. Her desire to live a life of prayer and poverty grew stronger.

It was spring of 1212. Clare was nearly eighteen. During that Lent, Brother Francis preached a series of sermons in the Church of San Giorgio. Later, when she met with Francis, she told him she felt ready to take the next step. He said, "Since you feel ready, Clare, the time has come to act. Will you come with me to meet the bishop?"

"Why?" she asked.

"To get his permission, so you can start to live the way we've talked about. You need the blessing of the church," Francis told her. "We can go there right now."

Hope filled Clare's heart. Her dream would soon be coming true! But then a doubt came into her mind. "Francis," she began, "you know that my father died recently. He wanted me to marry. Now my Uncle Monaldo is the head of the family. He, too, wants marriage for me. I'm afraid he'll make trouble."

"That's why we must have the bishop's consent—and protection," Francis explained.

They walked to the bishop's house. A servant came and led them to the room where the bishop waited.

"Peace and all good, Bishop Guido!" Francis bowed low. "I bring the Lady Clare."

Clare came forward and curtsied. "I am honored, Your Excellency," she said.

The bishop smiled and asked, "What is it you want, Lady Clare?"

"I want to follow Jesus Christ and live a poor life. I want to do what he said in the Gospel: 'Sell all you have and come follow me.'"

The bishop nodded. "There are many convents you can enter."

"I know that, Your Excellency," Clare replied. "But even convents have many goods. I want nothing of this earth. I only want the riches found in the love of Jesus."

Francis added, "We want your permission to allow Clare to live as the friars do. In time, more holy women will join her. I've made some space for them at the Church of San Damiano. They will not go out begging as mendicants—that wouldn't be safe for women—but will be enclosed. That is, they will pray and do penance away from the rest of the world. The friars will provide food for them."

The bishop replied, "For my part, I'm very willing to give you this permission. But what about your family, Clare? I've heard that your uncle wants you to marry a rich husband."

"Yes, it's true. But I know that if I follow what Jesus wants of me, he'll help me deal with my family."

"You are certainly a determined young woman!" Bishop Guido said. He stayed silent for a moment, tapping his fingers on the table. Finally he spoke again.

"I have an idea," he said. "I need to think about this a little more. This is how I'll let you know what I decide. Next week, when you come to Mass on Palm Sunday, don't come up to take a palm branch. Instead, if my answer is yes, I'll come over to you and hand you a palm myself. That will signal that you have my permission to embrace this new way of life. If not, I won't come over to you."

Clare agreed. Palm Sunday was only a few days away. It looked as if her dream might come true. But she couldn't help but worry. What would the bishop decide?

7

PALM SUNDAY

On Palm Sunday, Clare was up early. She could hardly wait for the bishop's decision. She got dressed and walked to Mass with her mother's ladies-in-waiting, Pacifica and Bona.

The three arrived at the cathedral and found places near the front. "I want the bishop to be able to find me easily," she whispered to Bona.

Now a priest was reading the Gospel. It told of Jesus entering Jerusalem. The people shouted "Hosanna!" to him, waving palms. After the reading, the congregation went up to receive their own palms. Bishop Guido stood in front of the altar, giving palms to everyone who approached him.

But Clare stayed right where she was. Her heart beat faster and faster.

The bishop handed palms to the last few people. Then he looked over at Clare. She held her breath. He seemed to be moving back toward the altar. But suddenly he turned and came straight toward her—with a palm!

"Thank you, Bishop Guido!" Clare whispered as she took the palm. It was hard not to shout with joy! For the rest of the Mass, Clare couldn't stop praying her thanks to God.

After Mass, Clare stayed in the cathedral to pray. Francis, too, was there, praying in gratitude. Finally she spoke quietly to him.

"I've worked out the details of the plan, Brother Francis. Tonight I'll leave my house by the side door. If I leave by the front door, the guards will see me."

"What, by the little side door? The door of the dead?" Francis asked.

"Yes. It's only used for funerals. The body is always carried out through that door. No one will see me. Leaving by that door will mean that I have left my family forever. And I fear that, in their eyes, I too will be dead."

"Who will accompany you?" Francis then inquired.

"Lady Pacifica has agreed to come with me."

"Excellent!" Francis said. "Some friars will be waiting. They'll escort you out of the city to the Church of Saint Mary of the Angels, the *Porziuncola*. There we will receive you as a poor follower of Jesus Christ. God be with you, Clare!"

Clare went home and explained the plan to Pacifica. "No one must know what we are doing, Pacifica," she said. "If anyone in my family finds out, they'll try to stop us."

"Yes, my lady," Pacifica replied. Her brown eyes lit with determination. "Don't worry—I'll be with you every step of the way!"

Clare waited anxiously for night to fall. What would happen if her uncle found out? For now she pushed that thought aside. *God will help me,* she told herself.

8

INTO THE NIGHT

"Lady Clare, you look beautiful, just like a bride!" Pacifica exclaimed. "That's my favorite gown. And the jewels in your hair—how they sparkle!"

"Thank you, Pacifica," Clare replied. "I want to be dressed as a bride, for I will be the bride of Jesus Christ."

She finished arranging the jewels in her hair and on her silken gown. Then she turned to Pacifica and said, "Please go outside and wait for me near the door of the dead. All those who leave by that door never return—and I will never come back. It pains me to leave my family. But I will have the joy of knowing that I'm doing what our Lord is calling me to do."

"Very well, my lady," Pacifica replied. She left the room.

Clare slipped through the darkened rooms to the door. *How will I get this open?* she wondered. Heavy beams barricaded the door. She managed to push them aside. But a large metal bolt held the door firmly shut. She tried to move it, but it wouldn't budge.

Clare knelt down and prayed, "Lord Jesus, help me to open this door. If you want me to follow you, I need your help—now!"

She got up and tried again. Slowly, ever so slowly, the massive bolt began to move. Clare pushed it with all her might. Finally it creaked open! She silently prayed a short prayer of thanks. Then she opened the door and looked out.

"Pacifica, here I am!" she whispered. "Let's go! No one must see us."

The two dark figures hurried silently along the darkened, silent streets of Assisi. Feeble flames of candlelight flickered in the windows.

"Look!" said Clare. "I see the friars just up ahead!"

Two men in dark hooded robes stood waiting on a street corner. As the women approached, they quietly greeted them, "Peace and all good! Follow us!"

The four shadowy figures made their way to the city gate. As they neared it, one of the friars whispered, "The bishop sent orders that the guards should let us leave the city through this gate."

Indeed, they were allowed to pass. "From here it's not far to the Church of Saint Mary of the Angels," one of the friars said.

They made their way down the narrow road leading to the small church.

"Look, Lady Clare!" Pacifica exclaimed as they neared the church. "Look at all the lights! And I hear singing!"

They entered the little church, where Francis and several other brothers were singing and praying. Francis saw the women and came over to them.

"Christiana!" he called to Clare. To honor Jesus, this was a name that was often used by women entering religious life in those days. "What is it you wish?"

"I wish to offer myself to Jesus Christ, to be his forever!" Clare replied, the candle-light glinting on her jewels.

"Do you wish to live a life of poverty, having only Jesus Christ for your wealth?" Francis asked.

Clare answered with a heartfelt "Yes!" She removed the ornaments from her hair.

Francis said loudly, "Come forward!"

Clare stepped forward and knelt down. Francis took out a large pair of scissors and began to cut off her hair. This was called "tonsure," and it symbolized a woman's dedication to Jesus.

As the locks of Clare's beautiful golden hair fell to the floor, Pacifica wiped away a

"Please sell these and give the money to the poor."

tear. She fully supported Clare, but also felt sad at the way she looked now. Clare's hair was cut very short, above her ears, in fact. But now Francis was handing her a veil to cover her head.

"Here, Christiana," he said, "take this veil. Take also this simple gray robe, a sign of your love for Jesus in his poverty."

Clare took the veil and robe as the friars chanted psalms. "How I rejoice to go to the house of the Lord!" they sang as she removed her jewels, handing them to Pacifica.

Pacifica held the large robe, which shielded Clare from view completely. Behind it, Clare slipped out of her dress as she stepped forward, placing her arms in the robe and tying it securely around her. Behind her, the heavy dress fell to the floor.

Wearing the robe and veil, Clare looked radiant. She was overjoyed that she had taken this decisive step. She gave her armload of clothes and jewelry to Francis, saying, "Please sell these and give the money to the poor."

Pacifica rejoiced for Clare, but she was also worried. Clare's family might have missed her by now. *What will they do when they find out where she is?* Pacifica fretted.

9

A NEW LIFE

The friars soon finished chanting the psalms. Francis turned to Clare and said, "We must go now. I'm taking you to the convent of San Paolo."

"I know it—it's the Benedictine convent," Clare replied. "But it's a wealthy convent. I cannot stay there for long."

"You won't have to," Francis assured her. "But for now, it's the only safe place for you. Your uncle may make trouble!"

The small group made their way through the darkness to the city of Bastia, several miles away. Just before sunrise, they arrived at the convent. The abbess came to the heavy wooden door and greeted Clare.

"Come in, my daughter," she said. "You are welcome to stay here until your family accepts your religious vocation."

Clare thanked the abbess with all her heart. Then she went to the chapel to pray.

Back at the Offreduccio household, Lady Ortolana was concerned. *Where can Clare be?* she worried. *Pacifica is missing, too!*

Later that morning, Pacifica returned.

"Pacifica!" Ortolana called when she saw her approach the house. "You're alone! Where is Clare? Has anything happened?"

Pacifica knew she had to tell the truth.

"My lady," she began, "Clare is safe in the house of God. Last night she went to Francis and his brothers. She wants to live a poor life just as they do."

"I knew she wanted this," Ortolana cried. "But it's hard to believe she's actually done it, even though she did give her inheritance to the poor. But where is she? Is she all right?"

Pacifica replied, "For now, she's at the convent of San Paolo in Bastia. But she will only stay there for a few days."

"The convent of San Paolo!" Ortolana mused. "At least they will have decent food and living quarters. If only Favarone were still alive!" she sighed. "He would at least understand what Clare is trying to do, even if he didn't agree with it. But what will Monaldo do? I fear the worst."

The news spread quickly among Clare's relatives. When Uncle Monaldo heard it, he jumped up and roared to one of his brothers, "She will not disgrace our family like this! I will not have an Offreduccio reduced to begging for food! We must go and bring her back home—now! I'll get some of the other men together."

It didn't take long to gather a group of relatives. Seven knights of the Offreduccio clan rode their horses to the convent of San Paolo and knocked on the door. The abbess appeared.

"Greetings in the name of Jesus Christ!" she welcomed them. "What is your business here?"

Monaldo bellowed at her. "We want Lady Clare back! Bring her to us right away!"

"I'll allow you to see her," the abbess responded. "But to go with you—or not—is her decision, and hers alone."

She ushered them into a small reception room, then left. A few minutes later, Clare entered, wearing her veil and robe. Monaldo's eyes blazed with anger.

"Clare!" he yelled. "I demand to know what you are doing here!"

"Uncle Monaldo," she replied softly. "I'm here to follow Jesus in his example of a poor and simple life, as Brother Francis does."

"Rubbish!" Monaldo screamed. "You're disgracing the Offreduccio family name! You must return home with us at once!"

"Uncle," said Clare resolutely, "I honor and respect you as the head of the family since the death of my father. But I'll only be happy if I follow what God wants of me. I have to obey God, not you."

Monaldo softened his voice. "But Clare, if you follow Francis, you'll have no security in life. No money, no food, nothing. If you really want to be a nun, why not just stay in this convent?"

Sighing, Clare responded, "Uncle, the nuns here are good, but they follow a different rule of life. God is not calling me to their life of security and possessions. He wants me to follow Jesus in a more radical way."

Nothing Monaldo said could change Clare's mind. "I'll go now—but I'll be back," he promised.

Monaldo returned three times. Each time, he bullied, pleaded, and threatened, but it was no use. Clare stood her ground.

Finally, on Friday—Good Friday— Monaldo had had enough. He spoke to the other men of the family.

"Today we'll go back to the convent, and we won't come back without her!" His eyes glared with anger as he mounted his horse and galloped off down the road.

10

SANCTUARY!

The abbess looked out the window when she heard the sound of horses. *They're here again,* she thought. *I hope this will be the last time!*

Monaldo jumped off his horse and walked up to the door. Seeing them coming, the abbess opened it and greeted them. "It's Good Friday," she reminded them. "This day is a day of silence and prayer. You certainly may see Clare, but please be quiet and brief. She will meet you in the chapel."

Monaldo and his men strode into the chapel, where Clare was already waiting. She was standing near the altar.

"Clare," he began, "today you must come back with us. We want you home for Easter."

Clare had a determined look on her face. "Uncle Monaldo," she began, "you've come here every day this week, and every day I've told you the same thing. I'm doing what God wants me to do. He's calling me to follow Jesus. Nothing you can say or do will change that."

Monaldo raised his voice. "Enough, Clare! No more arguing! If you won't come with us willingly, I'll take you by force."

He stepped forward, his face flushed with anger. Clare could tell that he meant what he said. The young woman did the only thing she could do. She quickly moved to the altar, clutching the altar cloth with her right hand.

Monaldo knew what this meant. "Clare!" he shouted, "I will not allow you to claim the right of sanctuary!"

In those days, when people went into a church and held the altar cloth, it meant they were claiming the right of sanctuary— safety. Church law prevented anyone from harming them while they claimed this right. "Uncle Monaldo," Clare replied in a strong voice, "you cannot violate my right of sanctuary. If you try to take me now against my will, you'll be breaking Church law!"

"I don't care about sanctuary!" Monaldo bellowed, his hand raised. Clare stepped farther back, still clutching the altar cloth. As she did so, a ray of sunlight fell on her. In that exact moment, she reached up and took the veil off her head. When she did so, the men gasped in horror. Her hair was shorn nearly to the scalp!

"What have you done?" Monaldo sputtered. "A woman with no hair is a disgrace! No man would want to marry you anyway! I'm through with you!"

In silence, he turned around and walked out. The other men followed.

Clare whispered a prayer, "Thank you, Lord! Even if they don't understand, at least they won't try anymore to force me to forsake my dream!" She knelt down and prayed before the altar.

The crisis had passed. Now Clare was free. She would be able to follow Jesus in a life of poverty and service. Clare celebrated Easter that year more joyously than ever before.

One day soon after, the abbess came and told Clare, "Francis is here to see you."

Clare went to the visiting room and found Francis and another brother waiting for her.

"Clare, it's time to make another journey. The place at San Damiano isn't ready yet, so for now we'll bring you to another convent, this one at the Church of Sant'Angelo in Panzo."

"That's fine with me," she replied. "When will we leave?"

"Right away!" was the answer.

Clare bid the abbess and the other nuns goodbye and soon found herself at Sant'Angelo. It wasn't long before Clare received a wonderful gift.

11

A WONDERFUL GIFT

Lady Catherine trudged up the road to Sant'Angelo. *It's been over two weeks now since I've seen Clare!* she thought. *How anxious I am to see my sister again!*

She knocked at the door of the convent and was overjoyed when Clare herself answered it! "Catherine! Welcome! How happy I am to see you!" Clare exclaimed.

The two sisters melted into a big hug, overjoyed to be together again. "What brings you here?" Clare asked.

Catherine looked thoughtful. A smile began to come over her face.

"Clare, I know you're happy here. I have been doing a lot of thinking lately. I've thought about all the things that you said, about how you want to follow Jesus. I, too, want to live like you, in poverty, a spouse of Christ!"

Clare was happy to hear this, but she didn't want her sister to feel pressured.

"Catherine, I'm delighted. But are you really sure?"

"Yes!" Catherine said fervently. "Certainly I'm happy to be with you, but that's not my reason for coming. I want to give my life to Jesus. Even if you weren't here, I would still want to do it."

"There's one other thing, Catherine," Clare reminded her. "Uncle Monaldo will be very angry when he finds out."

"I know," Catherine replied. "I heard about how he went to the convent of San Paolo and tried to drag you away."

"Yes, I'm sure he'll try it again. But we'll trust in God to help us."

Catherine settled right in, happy to wear a poor robe and give up her fine clothes. But Clare was right. It wasn't long before their uncle Monaldo heard that another niece had gone off to be a nun.

"I will not have another member of the Offreduccio family going off to follow that crazy Francis!" Monaldo shouted when he heard the news. Once again, he gathered a group of men, and off they rode to Panzo.

They pounded on the door of the convent. One of the nuns led them into the garden where they waited. When Clare and Catherine appeared, Monaldo wouldn't even look at Clare. He shouted at Catherine,

"Come back home! Isn't it enough that your sister has chosen to waste her life?"

Catherine's heart pounded, but she replied in a strong voice, "You can't make me leave, Uncle. I'm giving my life to Jesus. Nothing you can say will make me change my mind."

"This time we won't rely on words!" Monaldo roared. Two of his men grabbed her by the arms and began to drag her along.

"Let me go!" Catherine screamed. But they held her tightly. Soon they were half-way through the garden.

Clare began to pray. "Lord Jesus, do not let them succeed in this!" she prayed out loud. "Stop them! Help Catherine and deliver her from these violent men!"

The men began cursing. Something strange was happening. They could no longer drag Catherine along the ground. She had suddenly become so heavy they couldn't budge her!

Monaldo was shouting at them. "What's the matter with you? She's only a girl! Are you such weaklings that you can't even pick her up?"

"Lord Jesus, help Catherine!" Clare prayed.

He started over toward Catherine and lifted his arm to strike her. But suddenly, he began to scream.

"My arm! My arm! I—I can't move it!"

His arm was paralyzed! Try as he might, he couldn't move it. Enraged, he could do nothing but call his men off. They rode away, defeated again—for the final time.

As soon as they were gone, Clare rushed to her sister.

"Catherine, are you all right?" she asked. Tenderly, she helped her up.

"Yes, I'm fine," Catherine said as she got up from the ground. "A bit shaken, but I'll survive."

"Come inside with me. I think they're gone for good. You'll be safe now!"

Some days later, Clare told Catherine, "Brother Francis will be here tomorrow. He will give you the habit and tonsure."

"Thanks be to God!" Catherine exclaimed.

When Francis arrived the next day, the three went into the chapel. Several other brothers were chanting hymns. Francis gave Catherine her habit. Then her hair was cut off, as Clare's had been, and she put on the veil.

"Catherine," Francis told her, "from now on you will be called Agnes. In Latin, it means 'lamb,' for, like a lamb, you are pure and innocent. You are offering your life to God."

12

TO SAN DAMIANO

Clare and Agnes were still living at Sant'Angelo. One day a visitor arrived.

It was Francis. "I have some good news for you!" he said. "You'll now have your own convent. San Damiano is finally ready for you!"

"That's wonderful!" Clare burst out. "It's been a little awkward living here with the other nuns. They're wonderful, of course, but they have their own life and mission. God has a different mission in mind for us."

"Yes," Agnes chimed in. "But tell us about San Damiano!"

"Well, you know that, with the help of others, I repaired the church. There's a small building behind it for you to live in. It's simple and poor, but you'll have all you need."

"How soon can we go?" Clare asked.

"Right away!" was the reply.

Soon they were on their way. After a few hours of walking, they were in San Damiano.

As they walked down to the small stone building set among olive trees, Clare turned to her sister. "I'm so happy!" she exclaimed. "What a beautiful spot. Here we can be alone with God and pray for the needs of our people!"

"What will we do about food?" Agnes asked.

Clare replied, "God will always take care of us. We'll never lack for anything we really need."

The two women worked hard to clean their simple dwelling. They gave special attention to the chapel. Day after day, Clare and Agnes prayed and worked, worked and prayed. Little by little, a way of life was beginning to take form. They began to call themselves the Poor Ladies.

One day they heard a knock on the door. Clare opened it and gasped in surprise. "Pacifica! Is it you?"

"Yes, my lady! I've missed you so much!" She stepped forward and gave Clare a big hug.

"Pacifica, I'm no longer a fine lady. Just call me Clare."

"Clare, ever since you left, I've been thinking. It's true that I miss you. But there's more to it than that. For a long time, even before you left, I felt a desire to serve God. I too want to live as you are living!"

Clare grew thoughtful. "Pacifica, are you sure?"

"Yes, my lady!" she blurted. "For many years I've been living as a penitent, but in my own way. I've offered small sacrifices to the Lord, I've fasted, and I've prayed. I've given money to the poor. But now I want to do even more."

Clare smiled. "We have a place for you here!" she said. "You can join us and live as a Poor Lady. Give it a try. See if God is really calling you to our life. We'll help you. Together we'll see what God wants of you."

Pacifica beamed. She took one small step over the threshold and into the convent. But that was the biggest step of her life!

13

THE COMMUNITY GROWS

Two dark-haired teenage girls were walking together through the cobblestone streets of Assisi. "Come on, hurry up, Filippa," Benvenuta called. "I'll race you to the corner!"

The girls began to run. They stopped, laughing, as they reached the end of the street. Benvenuta had won.

As they turned the corner, they found themselves near the marketplace. They wandered through the area, stopping to buy some oranges.

Benvenuta grew thoughtful. "Filippa," she said, "have you heard the stories about Lady Clare?"

"Yes," her friend replied. "Some people say she's crazy. Her uncle has disowned her for leaving the family and going to follow a beggar."

"But surely not everyone thinks that—or do they?" Benvenuta asked.

"Well, no," Filippa responded. "Others say she's doing something new and great in the Church. Many convents are rich, but

Clare will have none of that. She, her sister, and another woman are living in a few rooms at San Damiano, working and praying. From what I've heard, they have hardly a thing—and no food except what people bring to them. Sometimes they have so little that the brothers beg for them."

Benvenuta looked around to see if anyone was listening. "Filippa," she whispered, "I've been thinking a lot about Clare. Last week I even went to San Damiano and peeked over the wall. I saw Clare working in their little vegetable garden."

"You did?" Filippa asked, her eyes big in wonder. "Did you see anything else?"

"Not really. Everything was quiet. It was so peaceful! I felt myself wanting to be there too." Benvenuta grew thoughtful. "Filippa," she said, "you're my best friend. I don't want anyone else to know. I want to join Clare!"

Filippa reacted with surprise. "What? You want to join Clare? That's amazing!"

"Why?" Benvenuta asked.

"Because I have been thinking that, too!" Filippa said.

The girls looked at each other. "Well, what's to stop us?" Benvenuta asked. "Let's go right now!"

The two set off for San Damiano. Entering the church, they went to the curtain that separated the chapel from the Poor Ladies' living quarters.

"The curtain gives them privacy," Benvenuta whispered. "During Mass, they open the curtain to follow the prayers. But then they closed the curtain again—so they can be alone with God."

They walked to the curtain and rang the small bell nearby. "I hear steps!" Benvenuta said. "It must be Clare!"

A voice greeted them. "Peace and all good!"

Then the curtain was slightly pushed aside. "What do you wish?" asked Clare.

A moment later the words were spilling out of Benvenuta's mouth. "We wish to live like you, Lady Clare, to be poor and to give our lives to Jesus."

"Are you ready to make sacrifices?" Clare asked them. "We often go hungry. Sometimes people can't give much."

"Yes, we're ready. I'm not afraid of hunger," Benvenuta said. Filippa nodded her head in agreement.

"Then you may join us. The first few months will be a trial period. It's a time of testing. By living with us for a while, you'll see whether you are really suited for this kind of life. If you decide you're not, you'll be free to leave."

"How soon can we come?" Filippa asked.

"Go back home and give away anything that you have. Then come back tomorrow."

The girls ran off and did as Clare had told them. The next day they returned—to begin their new lives.

14

THE FOURTH LATERAN COUNCIL

The year was 1215. One morning at the sisters' weekly meeting, Clare told her little group of nuns, "Sisters, let us pray for Brother Francis. He's been asked to attend an important meeting in Rome, the Fourth Lateran Council. It's been called by Pope Innocent III."

"What's it for?" asked Filippa.

"The pope wants all the bishops to meet so he can ask their advice about some problems in the Church. He's asked many religious brothers and priests to attend, too. That's why Francis is going. It will begin in November."

Finally November arrived. Clare asked the sisters to say special prayers. "At the Council," she told them, "Francis will be showing the pope the form of life that we follow. We must pray that our way of living the Gospel is authorized and blessed by the Holy Father!"

Soon it was December. The weather grew cold, and a sharp wind howled. Advent had begun, and there had been no word from

Francis. The sisters fasted and prayed that he would be safe on the long walk from Rome to Assisi.

At last, one day in December, Francis returned!

"Peace and all good!" he greeted Clare and the sisters. They were all gathered in the chapel, where the curtain between the chapel and the sisters' quarters had been pushed aside.

"Greetings, Brother Francis!" Clare welcomed him. "I'm happy to know you've returned. What news do you bring?"

"We bring the prayers and greetings of the pope!" he replied. "He spoke about the beauty of Jesus' cross and our salvation through it. He showed us a special form of the cross, called the 'tau' cross. It's very simple; it looks like the letter 'T.'"

"The pope said those who are marked with this sign will obtain the mercy of God. They will live like Jesus, for this cross is his. When I heard those words, I knew that I would use this special form of the cross always."

Francis held out the cross and said, "Here it is, Clare. I brought it for you. Keep it in a place of honor."

Clare picked up the cross and kissed it reverently.

"We will always honor it," Clare told Francis. "But what did the Council decide about the poverty we want to embrace?"

A worried look appeared on Francis's face. He paused a moment and then began.

"Clare, the council is concerned about the number of new religious orders. The bishops think there are already enough of them in the Church. Rather than allow a lot of small groups with few members, they say that people should join the orders that already exist." Francis paused. "The council said that no new rules of life will be approved."

The sisters gasped. "What?" Clare cried. "Where does that leave us? We've been following the form of poverty you gave us. Can't we continue?"

Francis shook his head. "No, Clare, I'm afraid not. The council said the pope will approve of new religious orders—but under one condition. They must choose a rule from one of those that already exist. It could be the rule of Saint Augustine, for example, or the rule of Saint Benedict, two well-established orders."

"But we can't do that!" protested Clare. "Those orders are allowed to own property. We don't want to own anything. We want to be completely poor and depend on God alone for all our needs."

Francis replied, "Clare, we have to obey the Holy Father. Don't you agree?"

"Of course!" Clare answered decisively.

"Then we must both accept this," he told her.

Clare paused and sighed. Then she said, "If this is what God wants of us, I can only say yes. We'll choose the rule of Saint Benedict."

Francis smiled. "Good!" he told her. "Then you will be the abbess."

"I don't want any titles, Francis," Clare replied.

"It's part of the rule of Saint Benedict," Francis told her. "The abbess is in charge of the community. But that doesn't mean that you will take on any special privileges. It means you will serve the other sisters in the poverty and humility of the poor Christ."

Clare agreed. "All right. It's not what I want, but I will accept it. However, I intend to write to the pope myself and ask permission to live the form of poverty we desire."

"By all means, Clare," Francis told her. "I will support you completely. And we'll pray!"

15

ORTOLANA

Back in Assisi, Lady Ortolana looked out the window. *It certainly is lonely around here these days!* she thought. *How I miss my girls!*

Just then her servant Bona came in.

"Lady Ortolana, you look sad today. Is something wrong?"

"Not really, Bona," Ortolana said. "It's just that the house is so empty now! First Favarone died. Then Clare left, and Catherine soon went to join her. A little later, Beatrice, my youngest daughter, went to live with them, too. And, of course, Pacifica is there."

"Aren't you happy they're giving their lives to God?" Bona asked.

"Oh yes, Bona, indeed I am. But how I miss them all! We often used to pray together and share the Word of God," she said.

The next day was Sunday. Ortolana went to Mass as she always did. The priest was reading the Gospel. In the reading, Jesus said, "It is easier for a camel to pass through the eye of a needle than for a rich person to enter the kingdom of God."

Suddenly those words went straight to Ortolana's heart. *Am I rich?* she thought. *Well, our family has always been well off. We haven't suffered from want or poverty.*

As she walked home, she kept thinking about the Gospel story.

A few weeks later, she went to confession. The priest was a follower of Francis.

"Bless me, Father, for I have sinned," she began. She told him her sins. Then she paused. "Father, I'm a widow. I live in a big, beautiful house. But now my three daughters are Poor Ladies. The thought has come to me that, perhaps, I could join them and live as a Poor Lady, too."

"Do you want to do this only to be near your daughters?" the priest asked.

"I've thought about that a lot. I certainly would like to be near them. But it's not just that. Something else has happened. The Lord has been speaking to my heart. I feel sure that I want to spend the rest of my life for God and his people."

"Continue to pray about this," he told her. "If this desire is from God, it will grow stronger within you."

Ortolana left the confessional. She prayed, asking God, "Lord, what do you want me to do?"

She felt that she heard an answer in her heart. "Go and join Clare!"

Not long after that, Ortolana gave away her personal possessions and walked down the hill through the olive groves to San Damiano. With great joy, she joined Clare, Agnes, and the others, and became a Poor Lady herself.

16

THE MIRACLE OF THE BREAD

Sister Cecilia was worried. *What are we going to do?* she thought. *This is all there is to eat!*

Cecilia paced the kitchen, trying to think of how she could make a meal for the community—with just one small, crusty loaf of bread. Just then Clare came in.

"Clare!" Cecilia told her. "We have nothing to eat but this one loaf of bread! The sisters will be so hungry. Now that there are fifty of us, it's getting harder and harder to feed the community."

Clare nodded. "The harvest hasn't been good this year. The brothers go out asking for food for us, but sometimes the people have very little to give."

"I know," Cecilia told her. "Just now, Brother Antonio and Brother Marco returned from begging and gave me this one loaf. They said it was all the people could spare."

"Brother Antonio and Brother Marco? Where are they now?" Clare asked.

"They're still outside the convent."

"Do they have anything to eat?" Clare wanted to know.

"No, they don't," Cecilia told her.

"Then go right out and give them half of this loaf. We'll use the rest of it for ourselves," Clare said.

Cecilia looked amazed. "But how can I feed the whole community with just half a loaf of bread?" she protested.

"God will always provide for us," Clare assured her, "and sometimes not in the way we expect!"

Reluctantly, Cecilia cut the loaf and brought half to the brothers. When she returned, Clare said, "Now cut the remaining half into fifty slices, one for each sister."

She doesn't know what she's saying! Cecilia thought. Out loud, she said to Clare, "How could we ever get fifty slices from this small loaf? It would take a miracle like that of the five loaves and two fish!"

But Clare only smiled, telling her, "Have faith, Cecilia, and do what I've asked."

This doesn't make any sense, Cecilia thought, *but I'll do it anyway. After all, I did make a vow of obedience!*

She took the knife and cut the first slice, trying to make it very thin. *I have to make it last,* she told herself. She carefully put it on

"We'll never get fifty slices from this small loaf!"

a plate. *That's strange,* she thought. *Even though I tried to cut it thinly, this slice is very thick!*

She cut another slice. Amazingly, the same thing happened. The piece of bread was very large! She continued cutting the bread. Again and again, she cut thin slices that seemed to expand as she piled them on the dish. As she moved the fiftieth thick slice to the plate, Clare came back into the kitchen.

"I see that the Lord has provided for us!" she said with a smile. "Let's bring this to the sisters!"

17

A New Convent in Florence

The summer of 1221 was hot and sunny. Clare was outside working in the garden, pulling weeds and tending the vegetables.

"Clare," Agnes said, "why don't you stop a minute and rest in the shade? Your health hasn't been very good lately."

"I'll be fine, Agnes," Clare replied. "But let's both get a drink of water," she added, wiping her brow.

They rested for a few minutes under a shady olive tree. "Clare," Agnes began, "I thank and praise God that he called me to this form of life. I'm so grateful that we can be together serving the Lord!"

"I am too, Agnes," Clare told her. "It is a great joy to me that you and I are here together with our sister Beatrice and our dear mother."

They picked up their hoes and began working again. A few minutes later, Sister Filippa came running out. She said to Clare, "Brother Francis is here to see you! He's waiting in the chapel."

Clare propped her hoe against the wall and went inside to meet with Francis. He was behind the curtain with Brother Leo. Francis greeted her in his usual way, "Peace and all good!"

It had been some time since the sisters had seen Francis, so Clare was overjoyed to talk with him.

"I've been waiting for you to come!" she said. "Francis, as you know, news about our way of life has been spreading. In several cities, other groups of women have come together as we have. They want to live as we do, following the poor Christ."

"May God be praised!" Francis replied. "I can only rejoice at this. The friars have been growing, too. It's a sign of God's blessing."

"I have a problem, though, Francis," Clare said. "Just recently I received word that a group of women in the city of Florence want to live in poverty as we do. They've written me letters asking for advice. They want to know how we pray, how much to fast, and what kind of work they should do."

"Have you written to them?" he asked.

"Yes, but it is hard to explain only in letters. I think it would be best if we sent a sister from here to be their leader. She could guide them."

"That's an excellent idea," he told her. "Do you have someone in mind?"

"That's just it, Francis," she said. "The most suitable sister to send is Agnes. She has shown great zeal and devotion to our holy way of life. But ..."

Sensing what she was feeling, Francis asked, "But you would miss her!"

"Yes!" Clare whispered. "I would miss her very, very much."

"Clare, of course you would miss her. She's not only your sister in the Lord—she is your very own sister whom you grew up with," Francis told her. "But are you willing to offer Jesus the sacrifice of being separated from her?"

"Yes!" Clare replied. "I've been struggling with this. It would tear my heart out to see her leave here. But if the Lord is asking this sacrifice, I will make it!"

Francis told her, "Clare, your idea to send Agnes to Florence is a good one. I believe it comes from the Holy Spirit. Trust that God will give both of you the strength to bear the pain of this separation."

"Your words confirm what I've been thinking. I'll ask Agnes to go!" she told him.

Clare returned to the garden. "Agnes," she told her sister, "I have something to talk to you about."

Agnes sat down next to her under the tree. "What is it, Clare?"

"We need to send a sister to Florence to guide a group of women there. They are already interested in following our way of life."

Agnes looked excited—yet worried. "Praise God!" she said. "Whom do you wish to send?"

"You!" Clare replied.

"Me!" Agnes said. "How can I leave you? I followed you here when I was still a young girl. You are my spiritual mother and my teacher. I've learned from you how to love our Lord Jesus Christ. And I would miss our mother, Sister Ortolana, too, and all the sisters."

"Agnes," Clare began, "I love you too, very much. And I know you love me. But I also know that you love Jesus more than anyone else. Isn't that true?"

"Yes, of course," Agnes said. "But the thought of leaving Assisi ..." She stopped speaking as a big tear rolled down her cheek. She wiped it away and said with a firm voice, "Yes, I will go! I promised to always do what the Lord asks of me, even if it costs me a lot."

"I knew you'd say that, Agnes," Clare replied with a smile. "You can leave in two days."

18

BROTHER SUN, SISTER DEATH

One day in the spring of 1225, Clare sat at a spinning wheel in the convent.

Sister Filippa came into the room. "Clare, are you making more altar linens?" she asked.

"Not right now, Filippa," Clare replied. "I'm going to make some special slippers for Brother Francis."

"Why does he need slippers?" Filippa asked. "He's always gone barefoot."

"Yes," Clare replied, "but now his feet often hurt him. Last summer he was praying on Mount Alverna, thinking about the Passion of Jesus. While he was deep in prayer, the Lord gave him a special grace. The wound marks of the crucified Jesus appeared on Francis's body—on his hands, feet, and side. The wounds are called the stigmata."

While she was talking, Clare's fingers were busily spinning the thread. Now she finished and stood up. "Please call the other sisters, Filippa," she asked. "I have some news to tell everyone."

The sisters soon gathered. Clare began to speak. "I have some good news to share with you. Brother Francis will be staying near us at San Damiano for a while."

"How wonderful!" Benvenuta said.

"We're very blessed to have him here," Illuminata added.

Clare went on to explain. "Brother Francis hasn't been well lately, and he's coming here for a rest. He'll be staying in a small hermitage near the chaplain's house that's attached to the church."

The next day, the bell rang. It was Brother Francis and Brother Leo.

Francis was wearing his habit, with a large hood over his head. "Clare, peace and all good!" he cried. Under the hood, something was covering his eyes. It looked like a bandage.

Francis continued, "Clare, I'm not in good health. Something's wrong with my eyes. They're very painful—they burn all the time."

"Can something be done?" Clare asked.

Francis shook his head. "The doctors have tried. But nothing seems to help."

Brother Leo spoke up. "He has to keep them covered because light makes them hurt more."

As she looked at Francis, a tear rolled down Clare's face. *I never expected to see him like this!* she thought. *He looks so pale, so thin and sick.*

"Francis," she said, "your hermitage is ready in the garden by the side wall. It is near the chaplain's house. It's simple and poor, as you like. But I must insist that you sleep on a straw mat. Don't try to sleep on the floor!"

Francis smiled. "Clare, thank you for all you've done! I'm very grateful." He reached out his arm to Brother Leo to guide him to his room.

"Wait," Clare said. "I have one more thing for you."

She gave him a small bundle. Brother Leo opened it and told Francis, "Here are some slippers for you. Here, I'll help you put them on right now."

When they were done, Francis said, "Clare, thank you for thinking of my needs!"

Clare smiled. "Francis, how could I not think of you? You've given us our way of life. You are the one who planted us. We're like a garden of the Lord, and I'm only a small plant in that garden!" Then Brother Leo guided Francis to the hermitage.

Another tear rolled down Clare's cheek.

Nearly a year went by. Sister Amata was cleaning the convent, broom in hand. Suddenly, a mouse darted across the floor. "I've got it!" Amata called out. She opened the door and chased it outside. "I'll leave food for you outside the door!" she called. "But you can't live inside our convent!"

Clare was nearby cleaning the straw mats the sisters slept on. How she laughed at Sister Amata's version of pest management! Then, suddenly, a wave of dizziness swept over her. She swayed slightly.

"Sister Clare! Are you feeling sick?" Amata asked.

"I don't feel very well, really, but I'm well enough to work," Clare said firmly, continuing her cleaning. A few minutes later, though, she stopped, leaning against the stone wall.

"Sister, please help me," she whispered. "I really can't go on."

Amata rushed over as Clare fell to the floor in a faint. Just then, Filippa came in, and together they brought Clare to her room.

For the next few days, Clare had to stay in bed. Amata came to bring her food. She had grave news.

"Brother Leo was just here," she said softly. "Francis is very sick. He has written another verse for his beautiful prayer, 'The Canticle to Brother Sun.'"

Clare knew about Francis's prayer. In it, he praised God for Brother Sun, Sister Moon, Brother Wind, Mother Earth, and all the glories of creation. But a new verse? What could it be?

"The verse he's added begins, 'Praise be to you, O Lord, for Sister Death,'" Sister Amata continued. "The brothers have brought him to Saint Mary of the Angels, because he wants to die there."

Clare's face grew somber. "I fervently pray that Francis gets well, if that is God's will. I wish with all my heart that I could see him again before he dies. Please ask Leo if that's possible."

Amata gave that message to Brother Leo, who in turn told Francis. Although he was very sick, Francis told Leo, "I'm blind. But I want to send a letter to Clare. Get someone who can write it down for me, please."

Francis dictated the letter, and Brother Leo brought it to San Damiano.

Clare herself was still sick. With trembling hands, she opened the letter and read it. She began to cry. The sisters asked her, "Clare, what does it say?"

Clare wiped her eyes and said, "Francis says we shouldn't be sad that we cannot see him now. He knows he's near death. But he reassures us that we'll see him again—in heaven. For that, let us rejoice!"

It was late in the day, October 3, 1226. The sisters chanted their evening prayer with heavy hearts. That night, at the Church of Saint Mary of the Angels, the angels came to carry Francis away. Surrounded by his brothers, he gave up his spirit to God. Even before the news reached the convent, Clare knew in her heart that Francis was in heaven. She spent the whole night in prayer, mourning dear Brother Francis. *I know he's with you, Lord,* she thought. *But oh, how I'll miss him!*

The next day, the sisters heard loud chanting and singing outside. "What is that?" Amata asked.

Clare knew. "The brothers are bringing Francis's body so we can say farewell to him," she said softly.

Just then, the bell rang. Clare rose from her pallet with difficulty. She went down to the chapel and opened the curtain. Brother Leo was there with several other brothers.

"Clare, we're on our way to the Church of San Giorgio for the funeral. But we know that Francis would have wanted us to bring his body here."

The brothers opened the plain wooden casket. Clare touched Francis's lifeless hand, weeping quietly.

"I rejoice that Francis is with God, but I mourn for us. We will miss him more than words can say! No one can ever take his place. He was everything to us, after God."

One by one, the sisters came and paid their last respects to their beloved Brother Francis. Then, in reverent silence, the funeral procession made its way into the town.

19

A VISIT FROM THE POPE

It was September 1228. Once again, Clare was spinning thread, this time for the altar linens the sisters wove for nearby churches. As she worked, she said to Sister Pacifica, "Isn't it wonderful that our new pope, Gregory IX, canonized dear Brother Francis last month? Now he is Saint Francis! Even though I still miss him, I'm so happy for him—for now he's enjoying perfect happiness with God in heaven."

"We always knew he was a saint," Pacifica agreed. "But now it's official!"

Clare continued, "Now that he's been canonized, we can ask him to intercede for us—to pray with us and for us. I'm praying to him for a special intention."

"What's that?" Pacifica asked.

"That the new pope will grant us the privilege of poverty!" Clare told her.

Suddenly she smiled. "Pacifica, I have important news, and I just can't keep it to myself any longer. Can you call the others?"

When the sisters had gathered, Clare continued.

"Sisters, it's unbelievable. We'll soon be having a special visitor—the pope himself!"

The others gasped. The pope! What an honor!

"Yes, Pope Gregory IX himself wants to visit us. Years ago, when he was still Cardinal Hugolino, the pope appointed him to visit religious orders and learn about their rules. So he already understands a great deal about the way we live."

The next day, the sisters worked hard to get everything ready. Around midmorning, they caught sight of a small group of people walking down the hill to San Damiano. It was the pope and others, including several priests and cardinals.

Clare, followed by the other sisters, went out to greet His Holiness.

"You honor us with your presence," Clare said as she bowed to kiss his ring. "All of us here at San Damiano welcome you to our humble home!"

"Thank you, Sister Clare," the pope replied. "Since I was elected pope last year, I've had so many problems to deal with. It's a blessing for me to visit this place of prayer and peace."

"Please come in, and we'll show you our home," Clare said.

The sisters showed him the little stone chapel first, and then the other rooms in the convent. The pope looked around the small rooms. They were certainly clean, but practically bare.

"Sister Clare, you really do live a poor life here. You have almost nothing. Do you get enough to eat?" he asked.

"The Lord always provides all we need," she told him. "The people are very good to us and bring us food. We have a fine meal prepared for you now!"

With that, she led him into the dining room with its wooden table and benches. As they ate, Pope Gregory spoke admiringly of the beauty and peace of San Damiano.

Toward the end of the meal, Clare said, "Holy Father, I have a request. Now that Francis has been canonized a saint, it's more important than ever that we follow his wishes about poverty. So I'm asking you for permission to own nothing. That is, we don't want to own lands and an estate to bring in money. Instead, we want to rely on God's providence to provide for what we need."

"This is what you have called 'the privilege of poverty!'" Gregory said. "That's something new! You want the privilege of owning nothing! Most people want just the opposite—the privilege of owning everything," he added with a rueful smile.

Then he continued on a more serious note. "But Sister Clare, this could cause problems. If you have no land or endowment to support yourselves, you may not have enough to eat."

"We trust that God will never leave us wanting," Clare stated firmly.

The pope looked around at the sisters gathered at the table. They were smiling and happy. *There is something special here*, he thought. *There is serenity, peace, and joy. They really do trust in the Lord to provide them with all they need.*

"Sister Clare, part of me is saying that your request is foolish. It's nothing but idealism. But there's another part of me that can only admire this desire. Still, I worry that you may go hungry. What if the people don't bring you enough food? The brothers have a hard time feeding themselves. They may not be able to beg enough food for you, too."

Clare looked him straight in the eye. "Holy Father," she began, "remember the Gospel. Didn't Jesus promise that if we seek first the kingdom of God and a life of holiness, the Lord will provide for our needs?"

Gregory smiled. "I can't argue with that!" He was silent for a while as he thought about Clare's request. He finally said, "Yes, I will grant you the privilege of owning nothing!"

"Thank you, Holy Father!" Clare cried.

"But you still have to follow the rule of Saint Benedict," the pope added. His voice was firm.

"Holy Father, we will do just as you say!" Clare replied.

In her heart, Clare whispered to Saint Francis, "Thank you for asking God to give us this grace! But I still have more to ask. We want to follow the rule of life that you gave us, dear Francis, not the one of Saint Benedict. Pray for us that one day it may be so!"

20

PRINCESS AGNES

Far from Assisi, in the country of Bohemia, Princess Agnes slipped quietly into the castle in Prague. It was early in the morning, and she had just come from Mass. So she wouldn't be recognized at the church, she had dressed in simple clothes, just an ordinary brown dress and black cloak.

"Princess Agnes!" her maid Sofia scolded her. "There you go again, dressed in those old clothes! You can't go around the castle looking like that!"

Agnes put on a beautiful blue gown and a jeweled necklace. She went down to breakfast. "Good morning, mother!" she greeted Queen Constance. Her father, King Ottokar, was there, too. She gave him a big kiss.

"Agnes," he said as they started to eat, "what's this I hear about your writing to the pope?"

"Well, father," she began, "you know that the emperor Frederick II has asked for my hand in marriage."

"Yes, indeed I know, and I'm not too happy about that," answered the king. "Frederick is a violent man of war. We don't want you to marry such a man!"

"Well, I wrote to the pope to tell him I do not want to marry Frederick," said Agnes.

"Good!" her father said. "We will find you someone else. Perhaps a good prince ..." his voice trailed off as he began thinking of suitable husbands for Agnes.

Agnes took a deep breath. "Father," she began, "I've heard about a holy woman in Italy. She lives in Assisi, not too far from Rome. Her name is Clare."

"Clare? What about her?" Ottokar said.

"She is like Brother Francis, who preached about holy poverty. She lives a life dedicated to God. She and her sisters spend their days in prayer, penance, and good works. I want to be like them," Agnes concluded.

"So what are you saying?" her father asked. "That you want to go to Assisi? I don't know about that ... it's so far ..."

"No, father, I'm not planning to go there. I want to start a convent here. A convent just like the one Clare has started. The pope has given his permission."

Ottokar looked disappointed. "But I've been hoping that you'd marry a fine prince. It would bring honor to our family."

"Father, I know this will disappoint you. But I'm tired of the things of this world. I want to love Jesus and give my life to him in a special way," Agnes explained.

"Agnes," he said, "you've already done much for God. You've built a hospital for the sick in Prague. Isn't that enough?"

"The hospital is very dear to my heart, father. But God is asking me for something more. He wants me to give him my whole life in prayer and penance."

Ottokar stayed quiet for a while. Finally he spoke. "Agnes, I know very well that you're a lot like me. When you're set on something, nothing can make you change your mind. I won't stand in your way. If it will make you happy, I give you my permission. You can take the money from your inheritance to pay for building the convent."

"Oh, Father," Agnes cried, "thank you so much! I knew you'd understand!" Agnes's brother, Prince Wenceslaus, helped her make all the arrangements. The construction would begin at once!

In Assisi, a few months later, Sister Amata brought Clare a letter.

"Thank you, Amata," Clare said as she reached for it. "It's from Prague!" she remarked. "It looks very important."

Clare opened the letter and started to read it. "To the most noble Lady Clare, from Princess Agnes of Prague in Bohemia," it began.

"My goodness!" Clare cried. "It is from a princess!"

"I have heard of your humble and poor way of life," the letter continued. "The Church here in Prague needs holy women, such as you are, to pray and give witness to Jesus. Can you send some sisters here? Several women here desire to live as you do at San Damiano. I have already built a convent."

"Praise God!" Clare said to Amata. "The princess wants us to start a foundation in Prague. We've been praying that the Holy Spirit would lead us to new places!"

The letter continued, "And I, Princess Agnes, humbly beg your permission to enter your order."

"Well, this is indeed remarkable," Clare told Amata. "Imagine, a princess who wants to live as we do. She wants to leave all her riches behind. She wants to love Jesus and live for him alone!"

"Thanks be to God!" Amata said. "But who will go there?"

Clare said, "Not too long ago, God gave us a convent in the city of Trent, in northern Italy. That's not too far from Prague. In fact, in Trent, people speak a dialect similar to the language of Bohemia. Many women have entered the order there. I will write to them and ask five sisters to go to Prague. And then I'll answer Princess Agnes, and tell her we are most happy to agree to her request!"

The sisters from Trent soon arrived in Prague. Agnes herself joined them as a poor sister in the Lord. It was the feast of Pentecost, 1234. The princess had exchanged her earthly riches for heavenly ones. And Clare's Poor Ladies were spreading into other lands!

21

THE SARACEN ATTACK

The months and years passed. It was a Friday morning in September 1240. In the convent at San Damiano, Sister Francesca paced nervously up and down the hallway. Rumors of war had reached the monastery. It wasn't long before Sister Illuminata came upon her and asked, "Francesca, you seem upset. What's wrong?"

"Haven't you heard, Illuminata?" replied Francesca. "There is a rumor that the Saracens are on the way!"

A look of fear passed over Illuminata's face. "The Saracens! Those are the soldiers that King Frederick II of Sicily has hired to fight for him."

"Yes, that's right," Francesca replied. "Frederick has been fighting the pope. He has sent his men north through Italy. They're attacking those towns that have been loyal to the pope. Everyone is saying that Assisi is their next target!"

"Are you afraid, Francesca?" Illuminata asked.

"Yes, I am. But let's trust God. Sister Clare has said she knows he will protect us!"

Clare, frail and ill, was on her pallet. The sisters had told her of the danger. Clare was praying intensely.

Sister Francesca appeared in the doorway of the room.

"Is there anything you need, Clare?" she asked.

"Not right now, thank you." Clare paused a moment. "I was just thinking about Sister Ortolana, my mother. It's been several years since she died, and I still miss her. I'm sure she's in heaven now, watching over us and praying for us."

"We have many friends in heaven," Francesca agreed.

Clare suddenly sat up. "Through the window I can see smoke rising over the hills near Assisi. The soldiers are nearby. Quick, call the sisters and tell them to come into the dormitory and stay all together. Help me walk downstairs to the refectory."

"But Clare, are you sure you have the strength to do this?"

"Yes, I'm sure! Get Illuminata—the two of you must help me down."

In the refectory, Clare told the other two, "We must have the Blessed Sacrament with us. Go to the chapel and get the box, please."

"Right away!" Francesca said. Soon she reappeared holding a small, precious ivory box that contained the Holy Eucharist. With great reverence, she placed it on a small table.

Clare got down on her knees to adore Jesus in the Blessed Sacrament. Then she prostrated herself, stretching out her whole body on the floor, face down, and again prayed intensely.

"Lord," she prayed, "look with kindness on your servants, because I am not able to protect them."

Just then, all three of the sisters heard a strong voice. It said, "I will always protect you!"

Clare kept praying, "Please, Lord, keep the city safe, too! Do not let them harm it!"

The voice came again. They heard the words, "The city will go through much danger, but it will be defended."

A feeling of relief swept over Francesca. *How little faith I have!* she thought. *Not like Clare. Nothing can shake her faith!*

Just then they heard noises outside. The soldiers had scaled the protecting wall and were running toward the convent! Only the wooden refectory door stood between the marauders and the sisters.

Francesca felt afraid again, but this time it was different. In spite of her fear, she knew the sisters would be protected. She kept repeating the words she had just heard, "I will always protect you!"

They heard the sound of loud ramming. The soldiers were trying to knock down the door with a large log. Clare said, "Do not be afraid, my daughters. We will not be harmed, so long as we wish to obey God's commandments."

Clare remained on the floor and kept praying. Her voice was strong and clear.

Then, suddenly, the noise outside stopped. The soldiers had stopped ramming the door. Something had frightened them— who knew what it was? They were actually running away!

"Praise God!" Clare said. "He has kept his word. He has protected us. We are safe. They will not come back. Neither will they harm the city."

And that's exactly what happened.

22

THE LAST CHRISTMAS

Many years went by. It was Christmas Eve, 1252. Sister Balvina went down the stairs. At the bottom she saw Filippa, who asked her, "How is Clare?"

Balvina shook her head. "Not very well, I'm afraid. She's very frail. The doctor has told her again to stay in bed."

"I know she'll be very disappointed," Filippa said. "She wanted to be present for evening prayer and the midnight Mass. She so loves the feast of Christmas!"

"I'm going to get her something to eat," Balvina said. A few minutes later she went back to the infirmary and gently knocked on the door.

"Clare," she whispered. "I've brought you something to eat. Please take it. You have to keep up your strength."

"Thank you, Balvina," she replied. "I'm very grateful to you for all you do for me."

Clare struggled to sit up on her straw pallet and to eat the little bit of food. "What time is it now, Balvina?" she asked.

"It's almost time to go to chapel, Clare."

Clare looked sad. "I had wanted so much to be able to go to chapel and celebrate the feast of Christmas tonight. But my body will not allow me."

"I'll stay here with you and pray," Balvina offered.

"No, I won't hear of it. I don't want you to miss Mass. You must go to chapel with all the other sisters."

Balvina reluctantly agreed. As she was leaving, she told Clare, "If you need anything at all, ring the bell, and I'll come right away."

After Balvina left the room, Clare was alone. All the sisters had gone to chapel. *If I can't pray with the community,* Clare thought, *at least I can pray here!*

She began to talk to the Lord informally, as she often did. "Lord God," she said aloud, "I've been left here all alone with you!"

She spent a few more minutes praying silently. Then she prayed out loud again, "Jesus, I want nothing more than to praise and adore you with all the others! If I can't be present in my body, at least let me follow along in my spirit."

Clare closed her eyes for a little while. Suddenly, she looked up. What was that she heard? It sounded like music—and singing!

Now Clare could see and hear everything!

"Alleluia! Lift up your gates, and let the King of Glory enter in!"

Clare heard it clearly now. Without a doubt, it was singing! She could hear the brothers singing in their Church of Saint Francis! That church was across the valley, at the other end of Assisi. But somehow Clare heard everything, just as if she were there.

Now Clare could not only hear, but actually see in her mind everything that was happening in the church. She felt a thrill of joy through her whole being. "Jesus!" she prayed, "thank you for hearing my prayer! Thank you for letting me be present in this way with all those who are praising you in the church!"

Clare wasn't alone after all. The Lord himself had found a way for her to take part in the liturgy. It was the best Christmas gift Clare had ever received!

23

THE HOLY FATHER

After Christmas, Clare's health kept getting worse. She had to stay in bed more often. One day, she called Sister Amata.

"Amata, please bring me a parchment to write on. I've received another letter from Sister Agnes in Prague. I want to write back to her."

"I'll get it for you right away," Amata replied. She brought the parchment to Clare.

"Thank you, Amata. Now I just need a little time by myself."

Clare sat up in bed for a while, thinking about what she would say. Then she picked up her pen, dipped it in the little pot of ink, and began to write.

"Dear Agnes," she wrote, "with you I exult and rejoice in the joy of the Spirit. I want you always to know the joy of living for God." Next she wrote some instructions on prayer and poverty. Toward the end of the letter, she wrote, "Know that I have written the happy memory of you into my heart."

Will Agnes understand what I'm telling her? Clare pondered for a moment. Then she added a bit more. "I bid farewell, my dearest daughter, to you and to your sisters in Prague, until we meet at the throne of God." Clare thought, *Agnes will understand. I am not going to be on earth much longer.*

Amata came back in. "Are you finished, Clare?" she asked.

"Yes," Clare replied. "I've heard that two of the friars will be traveling north to Prague. They'll take the letter. Please give it to them when they come."

She was silent for a while. Then she said, "I want to give a blessing to all our sisters." On another scrap of parchment, she began to write again.

When she finished, she asked that the whole community gather together. Then she read her blessing: "I bless you and all those who will come after you, in life and after my death. As much as I can, and more than I can. Always love God and each other. Be faithful to carry out what you have promised the Lord."

The sisters started to cry.

Clare was growing weaker. It was early August 1253. Two years earlier, Sister Agnes, Clare's own sister, had returned to San Damiano from Florence, where she had lived for many years. The foundation there had grown and could carry on without Agnes's guidance.

Agnes kept watch by Clare's bedside day and night. "Clare," she said, "can you eat a little? You haven't had anything for over a week now."

Clare managed to shake her head no. "I can't eat anything, Agnes. My body would just reject it."

Just then, Amata came running in. "Clare!" she said excitedly. "We have visitors! It is the Holy Father himself, Pope Innocent IV. He has just arrived—he's come to see you!"

"Thanks be to God for this grace!" Clare whispered. Just then, the pope came into the room.

"Sister Clare, my dear friend," he said. "I heard that you are ill. I have come to give you my blessing."

"I would like to receive the last sacraments," Clare told him. Then she confessed her sins. The pope gave her absolution, and she received Holy Communion.

After Communion, Clare said, "I have one request to make of you, Holy Father. As you know, for all these years, the rule of life we've been following is the Benedictine one, as Pope Gregory IX instructed us twenty-five years ago. But I've written our form of life. It's based on what our holy founder, Saint Francis, taught us. I want to ask you one last time for permission for our order to follow this way of living the Gospel."

The pope looked thoughtful. "This is a serious matter, Clare. I've already told you that I think this rule is too radical. I read it last year when you sent me a copy. I haven't approved it because I have serious doubts about living in such total dependence on God."

"Please, this is the one thing on earth I most want to leave for my sisters. Please, Holy Father, reconsider your decision," Clare pleaded.

The pope looked at Clare, who was on the point of death. *How can I disappoint her?* he thought. *But I fear that this rule will be too hard for the sisters to observe.* "I will read it," the pope told Clare. "But I'm not promising you anything!" Then he left the convent.

It was August 9. Pope Innocent sat in his room, reading the rule Clare had given him. *Clare's request is highly unusual,* he thought. *Not only is her rule very strict, but it has been the common practice for nuns to follow the rule of Saint Benedict. Should I make an exception for this order?*

He knelt down and prayed. "Lord, give me light. Is this your will?" He picked up his pen, then put it down again. He got up and paced around then room, then knelt. "Lord, what do you want for these sisters?"

The pope shook his head and sighed. He picked up the pen. He hesitated. *Lord, what shall I do?*

24

FINAL GLORY

It was August 11, 1253. Silence fell over the room where Clare lay ill in bed. Some of the friars had come, Brothers Angelo, Leo, Juniper, and Raynaldo. They were praying.

One by one, the sisters of San Damiano came up and said farewell to Clare—Agnes, Balvina, Amata, Benedetta, Benvenuta, Filippa, Beatrice, and the others. In tears, Agnes said, "Clare, I'll miss you so much! How can I ever thank you for all you have done for me?"

Weakened from her illness, Clare could not sit up. But she smiled and whispered, "Agnes, the Lord himself will console you after I am gone."

Just then, they all heard the bell ring. Filippa went to see who was there. She returned a little while later, holding a parchment in her hand.

"Filippa, what is that?" Clare asked.

"A messenger came from the pope. He brought this and said you must read it right away."

"Please read it to me," Clare said with a trembling voice. "I am too weak to do it myself."

Filippa began to read the document. "The form of life of the Order of Poor Sisters is this: To observe the Holy Gospel of our Lord Jesus Christ ..." The sisters listened intently as she read on. Then they gasped. The pope had approved Clare's rule! Taking the parchment in her hands, Clare kissed it over and over.

"Thanks be to God, the Father of mercies!" she cried. "I have desired this for so long. Now I can die in peace!"

Everyone in the room began to sing hymns. Clare was drifting off. Suddenly she raised her head and looked intently across the room. She said in a strong voice, "Do you see the King of Glory, whom I see?" Then she closed her eyes in peace. God had taken her home to heaven.

The people in Assisi and the nearby areas already knew that Clare was a saint. Clare's body was placed in the Church of San Giorgio until a shrine could be built. On September 26, 1255, only two years after she died, Pope Alexander IV canonized her. In 1260, the people of Assisi finished building a church in her honor, the Basilica of Saint Clare. On October 3 of that year, Clare's body was brought to the church and buried deep beneath the high altar. It remained there for more than 600 years. Finally, in 1872, Clare's body was transferred to a special shrine in another area of the basilica, where it can be seen today.

Just three months after Clare's death, her beloved sister Agnes died also. She was canonized as Saint Agnes of Assisi in 1753. And in 1989, Clare's dear friend in Prague, Princess Agnes, was declared Saint Agnes of Bohemia by Pope John Paul II.

In 1958, Pope Piux XII named Saint Clare the patron saint of television! That was because of the Christmas Eve when she was too sick to get up for prayers but could hear and see the liturgy at the friars' church across the valley, just as if she were there.

Pope Urban IV changed the name of the Order of Poor Sisters to the Order of Saint Clare in 1263. They became known informally as the Poor Clare Nuns. Today there are about 18,000 Poor Clares in more than seventy countries. Saint Clare has indeed become "a light for all the world!"

PRAYER

Saint Clare, you loved Jesus so much that you gave your whole life to him. While you were still a young woman, you chose a life of poverty, so only Jesus would be your treasure. You wanted to spread the love of Jesus through the whole world. Even though you never left your convent, your heart was so big that you included everyone in your prayers. Your life was like a great light that still shines on us today. But you never wanted to draw attention to yourself. Instead, you thought of yourself as a little plant in God's garden. Through the beauty of your life, you gave glory to God.

Teach me to value the things that are really important in life, things like love of God and love for my family and friends. Help me to remember the needs of other people, especially those who don't have as much as I do. Help me to be generous in sharing with them. Saint Clare, you and Saint Francis were great friends. You helped each other to become holy. I also want to have good friends in my life. Teach me how to be a good friend to others, so that together we will live as Jesus wants us to. Amen.

GLOSSARY

1. **abbess**—the woman superior who governs and serves a monastery of nuns. A male superior who serves and governs a religious community of men is called an abbot.

2. **absolution**—the forgiveness of sin through the sacrament of Reconciliation when we are truly sorry. The priest says the words of absolution in the name of Jesus, who died so that our sins would be forgiven. We are pardoned through the power Jesus entrusted to the Church.

3. **canonization**—the ceremony in which the pope officially declares that someone is a saint in heaven. To canonize someone is to recognize that he or she has lived a life of heroic virtue, is worthy of imitation, and can intercede for others. Like beatification, which it follows, canonization requires a miracle resulting from the holy person's prayers to God.

4. **dormitory**—A room providing sleeping quarters for a number of persons.

5. **enclosure**—according to Church law, the part of a monastery or convent separated as the living quarters of the religious, which a person may leave or gain entrance to only by special permission. Religious orders like the Poor Clares chose to be enclosed in order to best accomplish their special work of prayer, penance, and devotion.

6. **endowment**—Money or property donated to an institution, individual, or group, often invested to provide an annual source of income. Universities, hospitals, museums, cultural institutions, and religious communities are frequently funded by endowments.

7. **fasting**—eating and drinking very little—or even, for a period, nothing—for religious reasons. Fasting is a symbolic act of penance that allows us to unite ourselves to Jesus' suffering and to help make up for sins. In the Catholic Church, those over the age of eighteen (and under the age of sixty) are required to fast on Ash Wednesday and Good Friday. On those days, they eat only one full meal and two smaller meals that do not equal a full meal. They do not eat between meals. The Poor Ladies of Saint

Clare and the friars who followed Saint Francis did penance by fasting frequently.

8. **friar**—a brother, or member, of a mendicant order. The largest orders are the Franciscans, Dominicans, Carmelites, and Augustinians.

9. **hermitage**—the dwelling place of a hermit, a person who lives alone in order to grow closer to God through prayer, sacrifice, and silence. Hermitages are usually very small and very simple.

10. **hosanna**—a Hebrew word meaning "save us, we pray!" It was used as a joyous greeting when Jesus entered Jerusalem on Sunday of Holy Week. Each Palm Sunday, Catholics repeat "Hosanna!" as palm branches are waved at Mass.

11. **mendicant**—A member of an order of friars who do not own property in common and who beg for their living. Mendicant orders include the Franciscans, the Dominicans, the Carmelites, and the Augustinians. In Saint Clare's time, women's religious orders such as the Poor Ladies chose enclosure in order to devote their lives to prayer and penance. They relied on food donations

from townspeople, but from time to time, a few sisters did go out to beg.

12. **pallet**—a small bed or mattress of straw.

13. **penance**—prayers, good deeds, or sacrifices such as fasting or giving up certain luxuries, that are performed to make up for sin and as a sign of one's intention to do better. As part of the sacrament of Reconciliation, the priest usually assigns prayers as penance.

14. **penitent**—one who does penance.

15. **Providence**—the love, care, and guidance of God over all of creation.

16. **psalm**—a hymn of praise. Psalms from the Bible are often prayed or sung during the Mass or the Liturgy of the Hours.

17. **refectory**—a dining hall in a monastery or convent.

18. **spouse**—a person's partner in marriage. Religious sisters take Jesus Christ as their heavenly spouse.

19. **stigmata**—a condition in which a person unexplainably bears the wounds of Christ on his or her body, usually on the hands, the feet, and the side. Saint Francis of

Assisi, Saint Catherine of Siena, and Saint Pio of Pietrelcina are three well-known saints who bore the stigmata.

20. **vocation**—the call of God for a person to live a certain way of life. One can be called to a vocation of marriage, single life, the ordained life of a priest or deacon, or the religious life. Everyone has a vocation to be holy.

21. **vow**—an important promise made freely to God. Members of religious communities usually make the vows of chastity, poverty, and obedience. Poor Clares make a fourth vow of enclosure.

Who are the Daughters of St. Paul?

We are Catholic sisters. Our mission is to be like Saint Paul and tell everyone about Jesus! There are so many ways for people to communicate with each other. We want to use all of them so everyone will know how much God loves them. We do this by printing books (you're holding one!), making radio shows, singing, helping people at our bookstores, using the Internet, and in many other ways.

Visit our website at www.pauline.org

BOOKS & MEDIA

The Daughters of St. Paul operate book and media centers at the following addresses. Visit, call, or write the one nearest you today, or find us at www.pauline.org.

CALIFORNIA

3908 Sepulveda Blvd, Culver City, CA 90230	310-397-8676
935 Brewster Ave., Redwood City, CA 94063	650-369-4230
5945 Balboa Avenue, San Diego, CA 92111	858-565-9181

FLORIDA

145 S.W. 107th Avenue, Miami, FL 33174	305-559-6715

HAWAII

1143 Bishop Street, Honolulu, HI 96813	808-521-2731
Neighbor Islands call:	866-521-2731

ILLINOIS

172 North Michigan Avenue, Chicago, IL 60601	312-346-4228

LOUISIANA

4403 Veterans Memorial Blvd, Metairie, LA 70006	504-887-7631

MASSACHUSETTS

885 Providence Hwy, Dedham, MA 02026	781-326-5385

MISSOURI

9804 Watson Road, St. Louis, MO 63126	314-965-3512

NEW YORK

64 West 38th Street, New York, NY 10018	212-754-1110

PENNSYLVANIA

Philadelphia—relocating	215-676-9494

SOUTH CAROLINA

243 King Street, Charleston, SC 29401	843-577-0175

VIRGINIA

1025 King Street, Alexandria, VA 22314	703-549-3806

CANADA

3022 Dufferin Street, Toronto, ON M6B 3T5	416-781-9131